# Enraptured

by

# RAPTORS

The Story of a Hawk Family
That Captured The Heart of a Community

♡

Photographs & Field Notes by

## JENNIFER PACKARD

Foreword by

## AMY HENDERSON

Edited by

## GABRIEL COUNASSE

*For Mary Ann, my guide, who introduced
me to the magic of raptors and so much more.*

First paperback edition September 2020

Cover and interior book design by Jennifer Packard
**www.jenpackard.com**

Library of Congress Control Number: 2020917339

ISBN 978-0-578-73724-9 (paperback)
ISBN 978-108-790220-3 (eBook)

Published by IngramSpark
Printed in the United States of America

# Contents

6

# Foreword

During the pandemic lockdown in the Spring of 2020, our Washington, D.C. neighborhood was catapulted into a parallel universe — a world untouched by epidemiology or ideology. It was a natural space where birdsong replaced rage-tweets.

Sheltering in place, we kept socially distant, wore masks, and learned how to wash our hands. The COVID-19 virus cast an invisible pall over everyday life, and a ghostlike stillness reigned.

But suddenly, the world of nature wrenched us awake and alive. A friend whose Kennedy-Warren apartment faces Rock Creek Park looked out his window and saw "a big bird caught in a tree." He spread the word, and neighbors rallied immediately to help. Dan Newton, a Kennedy-Warren resident and longtime staffer at the next-door National Zoo, called Zoo colleagues that were working during the lockdown, and soon a group was standing behind the apartment building in the Rock Creek woods that borders the Zoo. Looking far above, they could see the "big bird" dangling from a tree, its right wing caught in a branch.

We discovered that the bird was a Red-shouldered Hawk. In March, a pair of Red-shoulders had built a nest on the Connecticut Avenue Bridge next to our building. The huge nest was lodged in the crook of a sycamore tree that was easily spotted from the bridge, and the neighborhood had happily watched as the hawk saga evolved from nest-building to egg-laying.

Every day, people stopped along the bridge to check and chat, delighted to have nature intrude on life in the pandemic. Instead of unease and fear, we could focus on Spring's inherent spirit of renewal. The mother hawk sat on three eggs for over a month. On April 20th, the bridge contingent's optimism was rewarded when the first chick was hatched. Two others popped out in the next several days.

The neighborhood's adoption of the hawk family became official when wildlife photographer, Jennifer Packard, gave them names: the mother was *Libby*, the father *Walt*, and the chicks were *Covid*, *Cleveland*, and *Dorothy*.

It was fascinating to watch both mates fly off to hunt and then glide gently back to the nest to feed the voracious young chicks. Red-shoulders are known for the balletic "sky-dancing" they perform as they soar high above their territory to circle for prey below. They are solitary rather than flock creatures, and they mate for life.

All seemed well until May 1st, when the father hawk was snagged in fishing line in a tree high behind the Kennedy-Warren. He'd been fishing for chick-food when his wing got entangled in fishing line in Rock Creek, and when he went to hunt in the woods, his line-wrapped wing got hopelessly caught in a tree branch.

As would-be rescuers from the National Zoo and the neighbors watched from below, the hawk made frantic attempts to free himself before resting, exhausted. For several hours, he just dangled from his right wing.

Then Suzanne Shoemaker, director of the *Owl Moon Raptor Center* in Boyds, Md., suggested an arborist team that could help, and the *Bartlett Tree Experts* came to the rescue. The arborist who clambered up the tree was a veritable "Bird-man"— he gracefully climbed the tree, stretched himself out over very small branches, and managed to get the large and still-feisty hawk into a giant leather sack. Then he floated back down and delivered the bagged bird to Zoo staff, who put the hawk into a carrying case for transport to the raptor center for care.

When it was clear the rescue had worked, cheers erupted from the windows of people watching from their apartments. Dan Newton, who had gathered Zoo colleagues to help, told the Washington Post's John Kelly that the enthusiastic cheers raining down on the rescuers was "like stadium applause!"

The fact that the Washington Post thought the hawk rescue was worth covering says a lot about how the idea of 'community' has importance even in troubled times. The Post's John Kelly writes a daily column on life in the District, and he understood how this neighborhood story injected a spirit of joy into the darkness of pandemic life. Kelly's May 6th column[2] featured quotes from various people involved in the rescue, including the National Zoo's curator of birds, Sara Hallager.  She explained that because the hawk's wing was "just completely entangled in fishing line," she decided the Owl Moon Raptor Center would be the best place for the hawk's recovery.

Raptor Center Director Suzanne Shoemaker described how they were able to remove the fishing line "totally wrapped around one of the primary feathers" before giving him anti-inflammatories for swelling, and fluids to rehydrate him.  The hawk was young and strong, and when he proved he could fly, he was released after forty-eight hours near the woods where he was rescued.

Meanwhile, back at the nest:  oblivious to her mate's accident, the mother hawk fed and cared for the three chicks on her own — and she wasn't happy.  For two days, she screeched calls that echoed throughout Klingle Valley — essentially demanding "Where are you??!!"

When the rehabilitated hawk returned, the family went forward as if nothing had happened.  The three chicks have since grown into beautiful juvenile hawks. The mother fed the youngest and smallest first to assure her survival, and Dorothy has emerged as quite a neighborhood favorite. She learned to mimic her mother's calls early on, and her dramatic vocalizing has turned her into the Maria Callas of Red-shoulderdom.

The first-born, Covid, was the first to fledge. One morning, bridge watchers saw him hop onto a branch near the nest and spend hours testing his flapping strength. The next day, May 26th, he flew to a nearby tree. This set a pattern his siblings would follow: one day of preflight flapping followed by lift-off the day after. The second chick, Cleveland, fledged on May 29th, and Dorothy launched on June 2nd.  The young hawks will stay near the nest as they learn to hunt and are expected to stay in the area to start their own families. This is *their* home turf.

---

2       *Kelly, John. "When a hawk got tangled in fishing line, humans came together to rescue it." The Washington Post, 3 May 2020, https://www.washingtonpost.com/local/when-a-hawk-got-tangled-in-fishing-line-humans-came-together-to-rescue-it/2020/05/06/2637d5c2-8fb1-11ea-9e23-6914ee410a5f_story.html*

In our disrupted times, the neighborhood hawk family reminds us that life goes on — *and that we're all in this together.*

## AMY HENDERSON
Washington, D.C.

*Amy Henderson is a cultural historian who specializes in media and the arts. As Historian of the Smithsonian's National Portrait Gallery (1975-2014), she curated exhibitions and wrote extensively on radio and TV, Broadway, Hollywood, and dance; today, she is Historian Emerita. She writes articles and reviews for various publications, and emcees "Classic Movie Night" at the Kennedy-Warren, where she has lived since 1975.*

Nest

11

# A word from the Owl Moon Raptor Center

Walt was a very lucky bird to have so many people watching and looking out for him. The fact that he was discovered so soon when he was entangled, and that we were able to find folks at *Bartlett Tree Experts* quickly (and they were able to respond promptly), are the key reasons why Walt's rehabilitation went so well, and he was able to return home in time to rejoin his mate to raise their young family.

We see many incidents of fishing line (and other forms of) entanglement and many raptors are not so lucky. People happen upon entangled barred owls, osprey, hawks, herons, geese and other critters along remote trails while fishing or boating, and we have no idea how long they have been trapped and struggling (or given up the struggle) to free themselves. If they are lucky and survive, these cases typically require weeks or months to recover from the muscle, tendon, and ligament damage that result from entanglement. Please make it your mission, while out on a hike or fishing along Rock Creek, C&O Canal towpath, or at the Bay, to remove what fishing line you find, and dispose of it responsibly. You will be saving the life of an innocent animal by doing so.

And many thanks to Jennifer for helping us to raise funds for the care and rehabilitation of our magnificent avian neighbors who fall victim to human activities. I am also grateful to all of the Connecticut Avenue Bridge "hawk fans" for their interest in this family, and for their vigilant and quick response to save the entangled daddy hawk, and therefore the nest of chicks as well, from a terrible demise. Instead, we have a *happy* ending!

**SUZANNE SHOEMAKER**

Director & President
Owl Moon Raptor Center
Boyds, Maryland

13

# Introduction

It was early March when we spotted a nest of twigs in a sycamore tree at eye-level, and two adult Red-shouldered hawks soaring high above the bridge. It was the first time I've ever been able to look into a hawk nest; typically, I'm several stories below with a crick in my neck for having to look up with a six-pound camera and lens. I knew a treat was in store, and I began to visit every day. The female hawk was usually there, incubating her eggs for an eternity, it seemed, but really for only 35-45 days.

The weight of the COVID-19 pandemic was getting heavier by the hour, it seemed, and the trip to the bridge became a high point, if not a distraction, from the impending uncertainty of the future. I could not wait for the eggs to hatch!  And once they did, I went two or three times a day to watch, learn, and document life as it unfolded before my camera. There's something beautiful, if not comical, about the fragility of a freshly hatched bird. As people would pass by, I would point out what I was looking at, and interest began to skyrocket. People wanted to know *what kind of birds they were*, *how long before they would fly*, and *what they ate*. I took it upon myself to learn everything I could about hawks. The more I learned, the more I wanted to share.

And so, these three little feathery bundles and their doting parents began to capture the hearts of all who came to watch, young and old, and all walks of life. The bridge in this story stands out as a metaphor in so many ways. In this time, when, "walls" are built to keep the other out, our bridge — offering its strength to hold us and provide a vantage point from which to witness nature and nurture — united people from different places, enabling connectedness and reducing isolation. It was a passageway for ideas and learning. I made friends with people I wouldn't meet otherwise.

Early on I named the hawks, more or less as a social experiment. If I told one person about "Walt", would the name come back to me from another? The father hawk was named after my dad, a WWII veteran who loved birds so much that he ensured they never went hungry amidst some of the harshest snowstorms in Upstate NY. He was the grocery shopper of the house, and I joked that every time Walt, the hawk, was away from the nest he must be at the store.

Libby, the mama hawk, was named after my friend's loving mom from Chicago, who raised three hatchlings of her own.

Covid was obviously named for the pandemic, a name that defined the times we were living in.

Cleveland, the middle hawk, was named for our former President and DC neighborhood (Cleveland Park).

And then there's Dorothy. On April 20th we noticed two baby hatchlings peeking out from Libby's protective wings.  As I stood and observed for a while, I later noticed a third rearing its fluffy little head.  In that moment of discovery, a woman was walking past and said, "What are you all looking at?"

Excitedly, we replied, "Baby hawks, and now there's a third!"

The woman smiled in awe seeing her first hawk, ever. I asked her for her name.

"It's Dorothy," she said, and I told her that the newest hawk we just discovered was to be named after her. She was so pleased that she said she was going to call her sister in Kansas to share the news.

My hope, dear reader, is that by having a personal experience with wildlife — or by looking at a photograph of wildlife captured in a way you haven't seen before — when you come across plastic or other refuse in nature you will be moved to take action and dispose of it properly. You may even recall Walt's story and his family, saved by the compassion of a community enraptured by raptors.

**JENNIFER PACKARD**

Photographer
Washington, D.C.

Jennifer Packard, "Hawk Family", May 6, 2020, The Washington Post

## MAY 1

### *The rescue*

Good Samaritans saw the hawk dangling upside down 40-50 ft. above the ground from a tall tree that was located near the bridge on the National Zoo's property. It was evident the raptor was in pain, entangled in fishing line, and would not survive the night without intervention.

The moments between the initial sighting of the injured bird, to the rescue, and the wait for word of Walt's condition and return, were tense.

"Have you heard about the father hawk's rescue?" and "When will Walt return?" were common questions on the bridge by a community of folks who were obviously entangled themselves in the outcome of the situation.

My friend Dan, who works for the zoo, told me that the keepers of the cheetahs and elephants, as well as the head veterinarian, were all waiting below the struggling bird, primed to assist, before the arborist came for the rescue.

Following his dizzying ordeal in the top of the tree canopy, poor Walt then had to endure his first car ride to the Owl Moon Raptor Center in Boyds, Maryland — a 45-minute drive in *good* traffic. I imagined him on that ride, in the darkness of his container, thinking about his family and the dinner he wouldn't be able to deliver to them that night. Walt would spend three days and two nights at the Raptor Center before his triumphant return to Libby, the chicks, and the concerned folks on the bridge.

Libby and the hatchlings wait for Walt's return.

Left:  Libby senses something is awry and leaves the nest looking for Walt who is being transported to the raptor center.

Above: The hatchlings huddle together, alone.

The north side of the Kennedy-Warren Apartments from which onlookers saw the hawk in peril and called for help.

## MAY 3

## The release

Walt is returned to the wild by Tina, a dedicated volunteer from the Owl Moon Raptor Center. The location is not far from the nest.

Walt

Hawk release photos courtesy of Dan Newton

"If we can teach people about wildlife they will be touched ... Because humans want to save things that they love."

— Steve Irwin

**MAY 6**

## Warm and dry

This morning it was raining and there was a chill in the air. I showed up at the bridge to find the mother hawk sitting on her young ones. Her feathers looked disheveled. The hatchlings, also known as eyasses, are covered in a white fuzzy down that doesn't keep them warm or dry so they need their mother in the nest to protect them from the elements.

**MAY 10**

*Mother's Day*

Happy Mother's Day to Libby who lovingly tends to her young! They will fledge (leave the nest) when they are 35-45 days old. Right now they are happy to be safe beside mom as dad hunts for their feedings.

## MAY 11

### A good system

Libby sits on the twisty branch above the Klingle Valley Trail. She holds a meal in her talons for the hatchlings. Walt and Libby have an excellent system. Walt is the primary hunter (or shopper, as we joke on the bridge) finding the food and cutting it into manageable pieces with his beak for Libby. Libby will often wait for him on a nearby branch several yards from the nest, calling to him with a robust *"kee-yeeear!"* which escalates if he leaves her waiting for too long. Once she hears him return her call, she goes to him (in an undisclosed location deep into the tree canopy) to pick up a piece of the meal to bring to the young in the nest.

One by one the mama hawk feeds the hatchings.

The process continues throughout the day, pausing only when the young grow tired with full bellies and fall asleep.

**MAY 12**

## Walt sighting

Today was a great day because I saw "Walt" (the male hawk, on right) in the nest with Libby. It had been several days since I last saw him, though from various sources I heard he was well and carrying out his parental duties.

A photographer on the Klingle
Valley Trail looks up at the nest.

Walt visits the nest to bring the young raptors a special treat: a frog.

Covid, the oldest, is standing tall and beginning to show his dark brown feathers. His siblings, however, have a little ways to go.

**MAY 13**

# Watching like Hawks

Every day the view from the bridge gathers more visitors.

"What's everyone looking at?" folks ask as they pass by, before returning the next day (and the next) with binoculars.

"Is that an Eagle?" a little girl asks.  "No," I tell her, "It's a Red-shouldered hawk."

She smiles and looks at the nest with child-like wonder, as we all did when we learned what we were looking at for the first time.  I think many of us are becoming junior rangers and naturalists amidst the pandemic.

A hawk-watcher takes a break from his work on construction of the new Bird House at the Smithsonian's National Zoo & Conservation Biology Institute.

## MAY 18

*Keeping nest*

Libby looks for fresh green sprigs of vegetation to add to the nest. Nest maintenance is continued throughout the use of their home.

Walt drops in to check on everybody.

**MAY 19**

*Kee-yeeear*

This morning Libby was gliding high above the tree canopy crying her familiar "kee-yeeear" hawk-talk. She was likely looking for prey now that the nestlings are a little older and can spend more time alone. Perhaps they feel content hearing her cries, knowing she is never far.

## MAY 20

## Growing feathers

Dorothy, the youngest, is becoming more like her older siblings every day. Her back feathers are browner in color, though there's still some soft down on her little head and chest.

While we call her "Dorothy", we really don't know hear actual gender or that of her siblings; however, it helps to have names to identify and refer to them.

The buzz on the bridge is how much stronger she seems, and surer of herself. I had to laugh when Mama Libby brought a small rodent to the nest and Dorothy aggressively went after it, attempting to swallow it whole. A cheer from bridge must have been heard all the way to Dupont Circle.

Covid

Cleveland

Dorothy

45

**MAY 20 (Cont.)**

One month ago today we discovered the hatchlings! The oldest, Covid (right), is showing signs of being a trailblazer. The first at everything and quite independent, he seems unafraid to navigate the world ahead of him.

## MAY 21

### Getting close

I nearly slept in an extra hour this morning, then realized we're getting close to 'fledging day' so I got myself together and ran to the bridge with my camera.

"Still three there?" I said to the familiar crew locked on the nest. "Still three," said a woman with binoculars wearing a pink panda mask. *Relief.*

Then suddenly, I heard an aggressive sounding Blue Jay and something fluttering in the tree canopy. It was the Blue Jay pursuing one of the hawk parents! The hawk landed on a branch and the Blue Jay began swooping back and forth, dive-bombing the raptor. The hawk just sat there, amused, watching the bird as if it was a show. The Blue Jay was likely defending its own nest from being preyed upon.

A little while later the hawk parents had a rendezvous on the twisty branch. They met for a break-fast hand-off for the young ones. Walt captures the prey, hands it off to Libby, and Libby will do a drive-by to drop the meal off at the nest.

## MAY 22

### Rainy day blues

In-between the intermittent rain I caught the hawks, drenched, amidst their morning rituals. This time, Libby sat on her branch and shook like a dog to dry off a bit. Later, she calls for her mate to coordinate feeding.

Left: Mama Libby calling for Walt:
"Bring me a mouse from the store," she says (in my head), "and don't take all day!"

Above: The little ones line up for their meal.

## MAY 24

### Out on a limb

Covid, the eldest, goes out on a limb to look down to the ground below. Soon the young raptor will be soaring high above the nest and the trees. But for today, a leap to a nearby branch is an accomplishment. His siblings look on with admiration and wonder.

"Ready world? Here I come!" says the young nestling.

Everyone ponders, "Will tomorrow be Covid's day to fly?"

**MAY 26**

## Cleared for takeoff

In a blink of an eye, Covid left the branch where he did his test flights, and made his fledge.  At first we weren't sure where he made his landing.

We looked hard to find Covid, and then we recognized his familiar face in a nearby tree. He didn't look fearful, in fact, he seemed confident that his mission went well. Everyone was proud of him.

"Where's our brother?" Asks Cleveland (above, left).

"I don't know," responds Dorothy, bewildered, "I turned my head for a second and the branch was bare."

**MAY 27**

*Welcome home*

Covid knows his mom and dad will be by for food drop-offs so he watches the nest below for deliveries. He has already spent one night by himself and is feeling positive about his abilities.

Right: Covids' siblings look up at him from the nes

Moments later...

Covid's first return home involved navigating a clear spot in the nest. It wasn't pinpoint, but he managed not to land on Cleveland and Dorothy.

"Welcome home, dear brother!"

He was just in time for dinner, which came shortly.

**MAY 29**

## Cleveland has left the nest

Today our middle fledgling, Cleveland, moved out, but it wasn't exactly planned. Here's what happened...

It was mealtime and the nest was crowded again. Covid had dropped in, Mama Libby was there, and of course Dorothy. Cleveland had been practicing his flutter jumps on the nearby branch all day, and when he saw it was time to eat, he was so excited he lept down toward the nest just like he saw Covid do just two days before. *But oh no!* The nest didn't have a good spot for him to land and he took a turn and a tumble, landing several yards below in a tree next door. His family was too busy eating to even notice.

The day became night without Cleveland attempting flight. Instead, he stayed perched on a branch until the morning sun would coax him into the air.

## MAY 31

*Sibling reunion*

Dorothy was alone in the nest until Covid and Cleveland visited with hope that mom or dad would drop off some goodies. They seem happy to see each other, rendering a beak tap. Behind them, Dorothy is more interested in her growing talons.

Dorothy

**MAY 31 (Cont.)** Our little Dorothy is yet to fledge the nest. Many say that they wish she would just live in that nest forever so we could continue to watch her everyday. Dorothy has a distinct personality: outspoken, quirky, and she cries a lot. However, these things make her all the more endearing.

Below, Daddy and Dorothy have a special moment together.

64

Dorothy ventures out on the branch (AKA practice flight deck) and looks surprised as her sibling unexpectedly lands right beside her.

"Watch where you are going!"

eft: Dorothy, morning person she is not. Her uvenile plumage is still working its way in on er neck. Her talons (above) seem to be rowing more rapidly than the rest of her.

## JUNE 2

### *Maiden Voyage!*

We knew it was going to happen any day, if not this very day. Dorothy, the youngest nestling of the Connecticut Ave. Bridge hawk family, fledged the nest today.

"I felt she was ready," says Sherree from Woodley Park. "She was out on that branch for a long time."

Several eyewitnesses reported seeing Dorothy on an extended northern branch beyond the nest. A little before noon, Dorothy scaled the branch further, using it as a runway to make calculated hops and flaps to test wind resistance.

"Ooooh! Woah!" could be heard from the crowd on the bridge as Dorothy became airborne several times on her ascent.

City buses whirled by. Dog walkers led their new doodle pups up and down the Klingle Valley Trail. The world seemed oblivious to history in the making. But the hawk watchers were fixed and focused on one thing: a raptor on a branch about to make her maiden voyage!

Then, at 12:51 PM (EST), Dorothy vacated the runway by thrusting her wings to gain lift. The launch was steady and direct. She made a perfect landing in a nearby tree several yards from the nest as onlookers on the bridge were heard cheering. Dorothy looked mature and distinguished as she gazed back at the bridge and the empty nest.

"She grew up so fast!" says Michaela from Cleveland Park. "Now I can go home."

Graduation is over, but the education continues for hawk watchers who look to learn what happens next.

News from the Bridge

Building Bridges
New Worlds

Tuesday, June 2, 2020

WEATHER REPORT

FREE & FREE

# DOROTHY FLEDGED!

### Maiden Voyage to Tree

We knew it was going to happen any day, if not this very day. Dorothy, the youngest nestling of the Connecticut Ave. Bridge hawk family, fledged the nest today.

"I felt she was ready," says Sherree from Woodley Park. "She was out on that branch for a long time."

Several eyewitnesses...

*Moments later...* Sometimes those pesky branches get in the way of your flight path!

## JUNE 3

### Breakfast is served!

Daddy Walt captured another frog to take to the nest but not before enjoying a little for himself. A passing bird flies by several times to discourage any hawk visitors to come near its habitat.

Below: Cleveland (we think!) waits for word from his parents about breakfast. He'll happily meet them in the nest, or anywhere, really.

he nest is empty when Walt lands with the frog, but not for long!  Cleveland swoops in and dad serves the frog with his talon.

## JUNE 4

### Empty nesters

Folks have been a little sad the last couple days after Dorothy's fledge.  She was the last to disembark, a few days after Covid and Cleveland were out the door. The nest, once fluttering with down-covered chicks and hovering attentive parents, is empty. The bridge, too, seems fairly sparse.

"End of an era," says my friend Robin.

"Are they all gone for good?" asks a mother with her young son.

The juveniles have embarked on a new chapter, but they aren't going far anytime soon. According to the *Cornell Lab of Ornithology*'s research resources[2], parents provide fledgelings vertebrate food for the first three weeks after they leave the nest, and may help supplement their youngsters' diets for eight weeks or more while the young learn to hunt on their own.

So, dear hawk watchers, while the nest may be empty, take a good look on either side. Bare branches are favorite perching spots, and you'll often hear mom or dad calling to them for supper.  They may go to them with a treat or entice them back in the nest (or elsewhere) with food to help them practice their flying skills.  Additionally, learning to hunt takes time, so we'll have a few more weeks to witness their growth and development.

2  *The Cornell Lab of Ornithology, Birds of the World. https://birdsoftheworld.org/
bow/species/reshaw/cur/breeding*

## JUNE 11

### Save a life, pick up trash

I was walking along Rock Creek near the bridge when something on the ground by the water caught my eye. It was a plastic netting of sorts. I wasn't sure of its origin or whether it was wildlife-friendly, so to be safe, I carried it to the nearest trash bin to properly dispose of it.

According to the U.S. Environmental Protection Agency, the most common threats to wildlife include both physical hazards from ingestion and entanglement, and toxicological threats from ingestion of contaminants attached to and trapped within plastic particles. Of all trash, plastic trash has the greatest potential to harm the environment, wildlife and humans.[3]

When I see refuse like this in nature, I now think of Walt and how something left behind nearly killed him and jeopardized his family.

---

3   U.S. Environmental Protection Agency, "Impacts of Mismanaged Trash", https://www.epa.gov/trash-trash-free-waters/impacts-mismanaged-trash#plastic

Left: Klingle Creek below the nest. Red-shouldered Hawks often build their nests in deciduous woodlands near rivers and swamps. The creek serves as a drinking water source, and for bathing when temperatures rise.

Please think of the image below whenever you encounter garbage on land or in water, such as plastics and Styrofoam. By doing our part to act responsibly, we could save a life, or maybe even an entire family.

## JUNE 14

### She wears her heart on her feathers

Sunday afternoon I took a nostalgic stroll to the bridge when I heard that familiar "kee-yeeear!" cry. I looked above the Klingle Valley Trail and across the forest of sycamore trees to follow the sound. Then I saw a flutter in the thick of the leaves when out flies a young juvenile making its way to the ol' twisty branch! The parents, Walt and Libby, use to sit there to watch for prey while keeping an eye on their hatchlings in the nest.

"Could it be our Dorothy?" I said to myself, hoping so.

The juvenile hopped along the branch, flapping its wings to maintain balance. Moments later, I heard a second hawk in the distance, and I look up to see its broad wings soaring in the blue sky. It was likely mom or dad checking in. The young hawk watches, too, calling back, then decides to lay down on the branch to take a nap.

As folks cross the bridge they stop for a moment as I point out the brown lump on the twisty branch.

"That's Dorothy," I said proudly to each passerby, as if I was pointing out my child on the softball field to another parent.

Then, in a blink, the young raptor flies to a close branch facing the bridge, and us.

Now at eye-level, there we were, looking at each other. I knew that the young hawk grew up with humans watching, and I wondered if she recognized me.

I paused for a moment, without camera to my eye, to take in the entire scene: the warm sun on the bridge, the rustling leaves in the wind, folks hiking the trail below, a little girl on a bike braking to see what I was looking at.

Left: The raptor stood in a curious pose with one leg up and the other anchored on the branch. It wasn't until hours later, looking at the images on my computer screen, that I noticed the little hearts on her lower belly plumage. Appropriate, don't you think? No doubt earned from all the love on the bridge.

# JUNE 27

## Dorothy's Ode to Maria Callas

I'm really embarrassed to say that I didn't know who Maria Callas was when my friend Amy referenced her the other day comparing her to Dorothy. Apparently, she and others have heard a hawk's incessant cries that sound just like our Dorothy (we're confident it's her because we've grown accustomed to her cry!).

I immediately scrambled to YouTube, my go-to, to see who she was talking about. Oh my goodness! This 'operatic diva' had such a beautiful mastery of tones, not to mention a wide range. In case, like me, you missed that day in music class when she wa introduced, Callas was an American-born Greek opera soprano (1923 - 1977), and one of the most renowned and influential oper singers of the 20th century. *Go Dorothy!* Who wouldn't want to be compared to this great legend?

his morning I was cycling across the bridge when I heard that nmistakable cri de cœur (passionate outcry). It was Dorothy on he twisty branch, calling to her brother on the other side of the ridge. *And it was passionate alright.* Four operatic acts about ood! I crossed to the other side of the bridge to find her brother ating brunch, pausing between bites to call back to sis.

Brava!" he cried.

)orothy takes a bow, tucking her head into her feathery plumage.

**Description:**
Adults have brownish heads, reddish chests, and pale bellies with reddish bars. Their tails, which are quite long, are marked with narrow white bars. Red "shoulders" are visible when the birds are perched. These hawks' upper parts are dark with pale spots and they have long yellow legs. The immature bird has less coloration on their shoulders and a tail that is indistinctly barred.

**Scientific Species Name:**
Buteo lineatus

**Adult Size:**
Adults are 16-24 inches long, with a wingspan of 37-43 inches and weigh 17-27 ounces. The Red-shouldered hawk is smaller than a Red-tailed hawk, but larger than a Broad-winged hawk.

**Clutch Size and Egg Description:**
One clutch per year, usually 3-4, sometimes 2. Pale bluish-white, blotched with brown and lavender in color.

**Breeding:**
Juveniles will breed for the first time around 2 years of age.

**Habitat:**
Bottom-land woods, wooded stream sides, swamps. In the East, nests in deciduous and mixed forest, with tall trees and relatively open understory, often along rivers and swamps. May move into more open habitats in winter. In the West, typically in riverside forest or in oak woodland, sometimes in eucalyptus groves.

**Threats:**
Deforestation has greatly diminished the Red-shouldered hawk's range. Other threats include poisoning from insecticides, pollution, logging, vehicle collision, and power line accidents.

# Q & A

**Q: What is a raptor?**

A: *A raptor is a carnivorous (meat-eating) bird.  All raptors share at least three main characteristics:*

> 1. Keen eyesight
> 2. Eight sharp talons
> 3. A hooked beak

**Q:  How can you tell the parents apart?**

A: *Female Red-shouldered hawks are typically 1/3 larger than males, evident by having more of a barrel chest and the males look slimmer.*

**Q:  What do they eat?**

A: *They feed on a variety of prey, primarily small rodents, amphibians, and reptiles.*

**Q: How long do Red-shouldered hawks live?**

A: *The oldest-known Red-shouldered hawk was female, and at least 25 years old.*

**Q: When will the young become independent?**

A: *A California study observed young hawks progress toward maturity. Findings:*

- Incubation period: 4-5 weeks
- Fledging: 35-45 days old
- Hunting insects: 7-8 weeks
- Catching reptiles, amphibians, and mammals: 10-13 weeks
- Independent of adults: 14-16 weeks

**Q: Do Red-shouldered hawks migrate?**

A: *The Red-shouldered hawk is one of 26 North American raptor species that are partial migrants. Mostly permanent residents in the west, south, and mid-Atlantic regions; northern birds migrate, but do not travel far. Some movement in winter as far south as central Mexico.*

*Taka Mahony, (age 4) wildlife photographer.*

*Found hawk feather courtesy of Michaela B.*

# Acknowledgements

I would be seriously remiss if I didn't acknowledge a number of folks who encouraged me along the way. Thank you, all.

**Mary Ann H.** for being my wildlife guide, especially for THESE hawks for whom you are owed the credit for discovering, and for being my greatest supporter of this endeavor.

**Joy S.** for being my #1 sister who sent me a pillow that says "Amazing."

**Uncle Larry** for carrying me on your shoulders to look for wildlife when I was a little hatchling.

**Helen H.** for my Peterson's Field Guide replacement, and for all of your interest and enthusiasm in everything I do.

**Amy Henderson** for writing a beautiful Foreword, and for being my mentor for this project.

**Robin and Pat C.** (my surrogate parents) for being loving examples to me in my fundamental years — and beyond!

**Shana D.** for sitting beside me in agriculture class when Mr. Cornell asked us what we wanted to be someday. *Dream realized!*

**Andrea W.** for buying a piece from my first exhibition, and for being my champion for three decades.

**Lynn P.** for chasing me down the trail and for being my friend.

**Sherree M.** for all the walks to the bridge, your motherly advie and enthusiasm, and for believing in me.

**Mary M.** for telling me not to rush this, and for all your great consult.

**June B.** for letting me into your apartment for a bird's eye view to take photos of the hatchlings.

**Thomas M.** for your genuine kindness and awesome video coverage!

**Michaela B.** for always being at the bridge and filling me in when I couldn't be there, and for the great hawk feather photo.

**Jacques P.** for inspiring me to become a better wildlife photographer.

**Colin S. Johnson** for taking my book picture on the bridge!  (Check out Colin's amazing work at www.csjphoto.com)

**Dan** & **Julie** for making that phone call which ultimately led to Walt's rescue, and for answering my questions.

**Suzanne Shoemaker** for all that your organization does, and especially overseeing Walt's care and return home to his family.

**Sara H.** for being that initial point of contact in the rescue, and for transporting Walt to Rockville.

**Tina L.** for nursing Walt back to health, and releasing him back into the wild.

**Linda** & **Brewster A.** for all the wonderful bird reference books which helped me in my research!

**Ed Norton** for reviewing this book, and for all the work you have done through the Conservation Lands Foundation.

**Smithsonian's National Zoo** & **Conservation Biology Institute** for support during Walt's rescue.

**Australia Zoo** & the **Irwin family** for granting me permission to use Steve's quote, and of course, for being an inspiration.

**Danielle** & **Gabriel** for your keen eye to edit my seminal book.

# Washington D.C. Animal Rescue Resources

## Owl Moon Raptor Center

Open daily 10 am - 6 pm
(301) 353-8947
https://owlmoon.org

Owl Moon Raptor Center is a state and federally licensed wildlife rehabilitation center specializing in birds of prey. Owl Moon cooperates with the Maryland Department of Natural Resources, Wildlife & Heritage Service, and local animal control offices and humane societies to answer calls concerning injured, orphaned, or otherwise jeopardized birds of prey. Owl Moon rescues, rehabilitates, and reconditions raptors with the goal of returning them to the wild.

## City Wildlife

Open daily 9 am - 5 pm
(202) 882-1000
https://citywildlife.org

City Wildlife was created to address the need for wildlife rescue and rehabilitation in Washington, D.C. Over the past several decades, urban development has reduced local wildlife habitat and wild animals have had to adapt to living in close proximity with people. Each year, hundreds of wild animals in the District are unintentionally harmed by people and the urban environment.

## DC Animal Care and Control

(202) 576-6664 (24-hour line)
https://dchealth.dc.gov/service/animal-care-and-control

The Animal Care and Control Facility is operated by the Humane Rescue Alliance under a contract with the District of Columbia. The facility is open 24-hours/day for those in need of assistance with animals, but has limited hours for those wishing to visit or adopt animals. The Animal Control Facility primarily houses dogs, cats, and pocket pets, but never turns any animal away. In the past, exotic species such as monkeys, alligators, and farm animals have spent time at the DC's Animal Control Facility.

# Afterword

Hawks soar high above us and have the ability to look at the world below with a big picture view.

In the spring of 2020, amidst the incessant noise of scary news media and fears concerning our health, livelihoods, and even our democracy, we were challenged to see the forest for the trees. As the virus spread, masks were scarce as we were trying to sew our own from old clothes. Grocery stores were out of bread, non-perishables, and toilet paper. Peaceful and not so peaceful protesters were taking to the streets in dozens of cities, and businesses were struggling to survive. Our nation, known for its *American exceptionalism*, felt like it was imploding around us.

Then one day, something aflutter in the trees captured our attention and quieted the noise: a hawk's nest with three eggs to hatch the gift of hope for all of us who longed for it. For a time, reality really was suspended, at least on the Connecticut Avenue Bridge. More folks were gathering everyday — albeit six feet apart — to catch a glimpse of wildlife in all its splendor. Conversation surrounded what Dorothy ate that day... How big the chicks were becoming... And the devotion of the hawk parents to the chicks. Nature took the main stage and we were in the front row.

Unknown to the hawks, the experience of nature peeping brought us a unique sense of community. All ages, races, creeds, and backgrounds of humankind were brought together. We were voyeurs to an unsuspecting reality that WE the PEOPLE are not that different from each other. We are all connected — each one of us and every living thing — despite the walls and ideologies that divide us. Even the hawk family loved and fought, left home, came back, and later became independent to continue the cycle of life. Sound familiar?

Some cultures believe that seeing a hawk means that the Universe is sending a message. This one, is loud and clear: Our acts of empathy toward each other and conservation toward our planet are the sustaining forces of nature and our existence. In other words, the big picture.

# About

Photo by Colin S. Johnson

Jennifer Packard is a Washington, D.C.-based photographer who has been published in The Washington Post, USA Today, The Wall Street Journal, Washingtonian, The (Louisiana) Advocate, and others. Previously, she served as a Public Affairs Officer in the Navy Reserves, and employed photography as a rehabilitative tool working with homeless women and at-risk youths. In her spare time, she volunteers her skills for Tregaron Conservancy in Northwest D.C.

Okavango Delta, Botswana

Photo by Mary Ann Hopkins

CPSIA information can be obtained at www.ICGtesting.com
Printed in the USA
BVIW120849011120
592281BV00028B/134

9 780578 737249